Distract the Brain: Manage the Pain
By
Dr Julie Winstanley

Table Of Contents

Chapter 1: Understanding Pain and the Mind-Body Connection   4

Chapter 2: Introduction to Mindfulness and Meditation   17

Chapter 3: Creativity Techniques   30

Chapter 4: Distracting the Brain: Techniques and Strategies   41

Chapter 5: Guided Imagery and Visualisation Practices   48

Chapter 6: Journaling and Writing as Coping Mechanisms   56

Chapter 7: Integrating Techniques into Daily Life   64

Chapter 8: Case Studies and Personal Stories   73

Chapter 9: Resources for Continued Learning   85

Chapter 10: Conclusion: Embracing a New Approach to Pain Management   92

Published by Dr Julie Winstanley

Chapter 1: Understanding Pain and the Mind-Body Connection

The Nature of Pain

Pain is a complex and multifaceted experience that extends beyond mere physical sensations. It encompasses emotional, psychological, and social dimensions, making it a highly individualised phenomenon.

For those living with disabilities, chronic conditions, or navigating significant life transitions, such as menopause and childbirth, understanding the nature of pain is crucial. Pain serves a key purpose, as a signal from the body, alerting individuals to injury or illness. However, it can continue, after the initial cause has resolved, evolving into chronic pain.

Chronic pain can be challenging to live with, impacting our daily lives and when it persists, can impede our emotional and mental wellbeing. Pain however, can be managed and its severity decreased, through the use of creative arts and mindfulness practices.

The emotional aspect of pain often intertwines with its physical manifestations. Many individuals experience feelings of frustration, sadness, or anxiety, as they cope with ongoing discomfort. This emotional pain can amplify the perception of physical pain, creating a cycle that may seem unbreakable.

By recognising the interplay between these dimensions, individuals can develop coping strategies that address not only the physical sensations but also the emotional responses tied to them. Engaging in the creative arts can provide a platform for expression, allowing individuals to explore and articulate their experiences, which can lead to a greater understanding of their pain.

Mindfulness and meditation techniques are powerful tools for reframing the experience of pain. By cultivating awareness and acceptance of the present moment, individuals can learn to observe their pain without judgment. This detachment fosters a sense of control, reducing the emotional burden associated with pain. Guided imagery and visualisation practices can further enhance this approach, enabling individuals to create mental images that promote relaxation and comfort.

These techniques can serve as effective distractions from pain, helping to shift focus and alleviate discomfort. The quote 'Distract the Brain; Manage the Pain' is so true, as by refocusing our attention in being creative, it can help you to manage the pain sensations.

Journaling and writing can also play a significant role in pain management. Engaging in reflective writing allows individuals to document their pain journeys, identifying triggers, patterns, and coping mechanisms. This process not only provides an outlet for emotional expression but also fosters self-discovery, empowerment and a sense of validation.

By articulating their experiences, individuals can gain insights into their pain, leading to a more profound understanding of its nature and impact on their lives. This reflective practice can be particularly beneficial for those experiencing life transitions, such as pregnancy, motherhood and the menopause, as it allows for the exploration of feelings related to change.

Ultimately, recognising the nature of pain as a complex interplay of physical, emotional, and psychological factors, opens the door to more effective pain management strategies. Creativity, mindfulness practices, and journaling provide valuable avenues for individuals to explore their pain experiences, fostering resilience and a sense of agency.

By embracing these tools, individuals can cultivate a greater sense of calm and well-being, transforming their relationship with pain into one of understanding and empowerment. The aim of 'Distracting the Brain; Managing the Pain' is to help you to develop strategies and tools through becoming mindfully creative, to learn how to best manage your painful experiences.

How the Mind Influences Pain Perception

The perception of pain is not solely a physical experience; it is profoundly influenced by the mind. The mind creates your perception of reality and of pain, if we can change the way we think, we can change the way we experience pain. Research has shown that our thoughts, emotions, and psychological state can significantly alter how we perceive and respond to pain.

This understanding is crucial for individuals managing chronic conditions, experiencing menopause, or navigating childbirth, as it opens up potential pathways to relief not just physical pain, but emotional pain and stress, through employing mental strategies. By recognising the interplay between mind and body, individuals can harness various creative and mindfulness techniques to reshape their pain experiences.

Distracting the brain is one of the most effective methods to influence pain perception. When attention is refocused away from pain, it can diminish the intensity of the experience. Engaging in creative activities such as painting, crafting, colouring or playing music, can provide an immersive distraction that helps individuals momentarily escape from their discomfort.

These activities not only serve as a diversion but also promote a sense of accomplishment and joy, further enhancing emotional well-being and self-esteem, which can contribute to a reduced perception of pain.

Quite often, chronic pain can wear us down, we can stop doing the things we used to enjoy and in turn, our self esteem can decline. Even five minutes of creating something, such as colouring or drawing, can foster a sense of having achieved something; facilitating a positive sense of self.

I would like to share my experience here, of pain, and what led me to writing this book. I regularly experience chronic pain, causing burning, tingling, muscle twitching and stabbing sensations, as a result of my fibromyalgia, arthritis and Functional Neurological Disorder.

On a pain scale of 1 to 10, on a 'good day', pain is around 4-5. On a 'bad day', it is severe, on a scale of 6-10, with 8-10 leaving myself bedbound.

On my bad days, if I am not bed bound, I do try to undertake five minute creative activities, such as colouring or use meditation, mindfulness and even tapping different parts of my body. These are all distraction methods and based on my personal experience, they have proved effective in helping me manage my chronic pain.

The aim of this book is to help you learn these methods, so you can also manage your pain experiences.

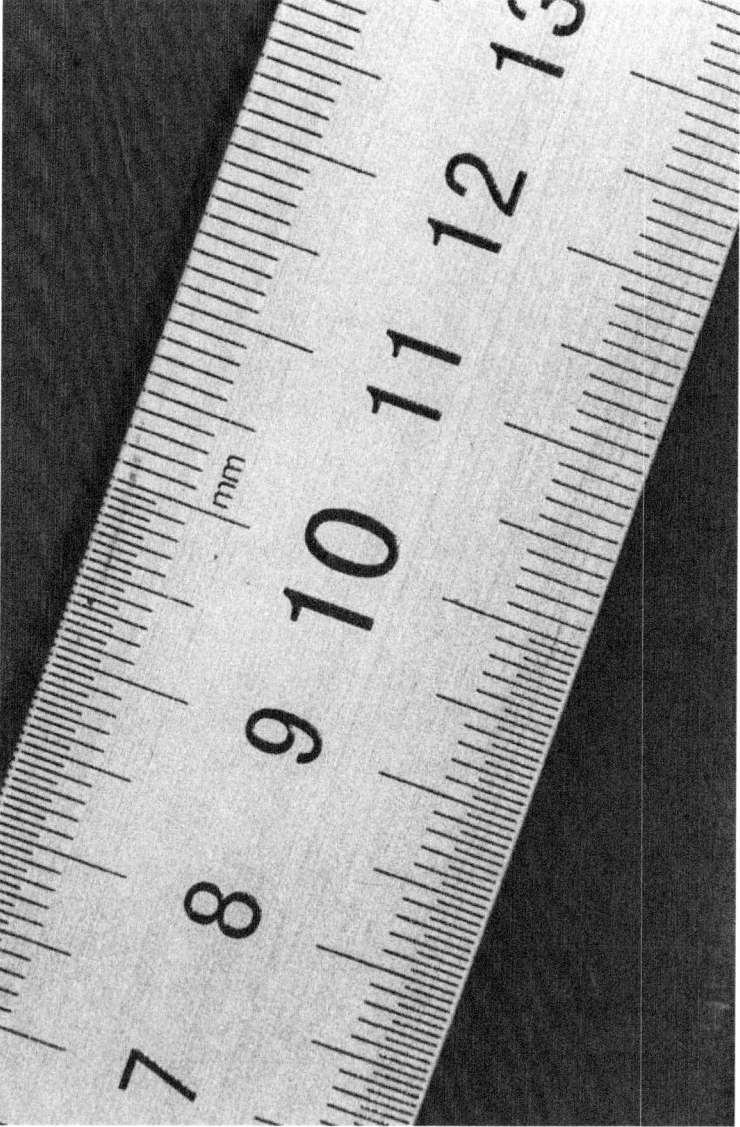

Mindfulness and meditation techniques, alongside creativity, play a significant role in pain management. By practicing mindfulness, you can learn to observe your thoughts and feelings without distractions; creating a space where you can acknowledge pain without allowing it to dominate your experience. Techniques such as deep breathing, body scans, and guided meditations can help cultivate a sense of calm and acceptance. This shift in perspective can empower you, to respond to pain with greater resilience and clarity, often leading to a decrease in perceived pain levels.

Creativity offers a unique avenue for you to change the way you perceive pain. Through artistic expression, you will be able to articulate your experiences and emotions related to pain, providing a healthy outlet for processing your complex feelings.

Whether you choose painting, writing, or colouring, these modalities facilitate a deeper understanding of how pain impacts your wellbeing and encourage healing. By transforming pain into art, you will find relief and empowerment, enabling you to reclaim aspects of their identity that pain may have overshadowed.

Journaling and writing are tools of being creative, providing valuable coping mechanisms, allowing you to reflect on your pain experiences and emotional responses. Writing about pain can help to clarify your thoughts and feelings, offering insight into triggers and patterns that influence your pain perception.

This practice can serve as a therapeutic release, enabling you to express your struggles, while also identifying what works and your successes. Over time, journaling can aid in fostering a sense of control and agency over your pain journey; reinforcing the idea that while pain may be a part of life, it does not have to define it or you.

The Role of Creativity in Pain Management

Clinical psychology increasingly recognises the role of creative arts in pain management, as an effective approach in helping people living with disabilities and chronic conditions, to cope with mental health issues.

Creativity encompass a variety of modalities, including visual arts, music, writing, dance, and writing, which can serve as powerful tools to distract the brain from pain and discomfort. Participating in these activities allows individuals to redirect their attention away from their physical sensations, thereby fostering an environment that enhances pain management .

Engaging in creative activities will facilitate a context or space for mindfulness and meditation techniques as a natural co-existing process; beneficial for pain management. For instance, activities such as painting or sculpting require concentration and presence, which can help to anchor you in that specific moment.

This focus not only diverts attention from pain but also enhances your body's relaxation response. Research also reveals the value of therapeutic touch in releasing 'feel good' hormones, such as endorphins.

The use of touch in creative activities, such as pottery-making therefore, can mimic the effects of therapeutic touch, fostering chemical changes in the brain, which send signals to your body, making you feel better, reducing your perception of pain.

By immersing ourselves in the creative process, we can experience a reduction in anxiety and stress, both of which can decrease the perception of pain. Further, being creative can be useful in also helping us cope with life transitions, such as pregnancy and menopause, by facilitating coping strategies to deal with stress, emotional issues and pain.

Mindfulness through the creative arts encourages a holistic approach to well-being, integrating the mind and body in active self-healing processes.

Guided imagery and visualisation practices can be integrated within creative activities to reduce perceptions of pain by providing structured mental exercises that promote relaxation and mental clarity. For example, a guided visualisation that involves imagining a peaceful landscape can be enhanced by artistic expression, such as drawing or writing about that scene.

This dual engagement allows for a deeper exploration of emotions and sensations associated with pain, creating a safe space to process your experiences without external distractions.

These practices can be particularly beneficial during challenging moments, such as when experiencing stress or chronic flare-ups, where visualising these positive images can aid in enabling a sense of calm, control and agency.

Journaling and writing also play a vital role as an outlet for making sense of our pain experiences. Expressive writing can serve as an outlet for emotions, helping you to articulate your struggles and triumphs. This form of self-expression allows for reflection and can lead to insights, particularly in understanding factors that can increase or reduce your pain experience. Journaling can help you to track your pain patterns and triggers, empowering you by, identifying strategies that work best for you. Different strategies will work for different people, depending not only on your type and severity of pain, but also based on your interests and preferences. By documenting your journey however, you will be able to cultivate a sense of empowerment and resilience, transforming your relationship with pain and putting you firmly in control.

In conclusion, by integrating creative activities into pain management strategies, it can provide you with a multifaceted approach, which can enhance your quality of life, whether you are living with disabilities, chronic conditions, menopausal symptoms, or need support during childbirth.

By utilising creative arts as a means to distract your brain, you can promote mindfulness, engaging in guided imagery, and expressing your thoughts and feelings through journaling. Through writing, you can determine, document and develop effective coping mechanisms.

This holistic approach not only addresses the physical aspects of pain but also nurtures your emotional well-being, fostering a deeper connection with 'self' and the healing process.

Chapter 2: Introduction to Mindfulness and Meditation

Defining Mindfulness

Mindfulness is a practice that has gained significant attention in recent years, due to its potential to enhance well-being and manage pain. Fundamentally, mindfulness involves paying deliberate attention to the present moment without distraction.

This can be particularly beneficial for individuals living with disabilities, chronic conditions, and those navigating significant life changes, as it enables you to truly understand how you feel at that very moment.

By practicing mindfulness, you can create a space in your life, where you can observe and connect with your thoughts and feelings without being overwhelmed by them. This ultimately cultivates a greater sense of control, self-awareness and self-acceptance.

Carl Rogers, discussed in his Humanistic, Person-centred approach, outlined the importance of fostering spaces where individuals can reflect on their thoughts, feelings and experiences. This enabled them to make sense of themselves and to understand what they need to do.

Mindfulness is aligned with such an approach. It offers a reflective space, where you can come to identify your own thoughts and feelings.

Mindfulness enables you to reflect upon why you think or feel that way and in being present in that moment of calm and relaxation, understand the impact of that state, in silencing those thoughts, feelings and pain experiences. The mindfulness state can help you to change your thoughts and feelings, by knowing you can control your state and dial down your pain experience.

One of the key components of mindfulness hence, is the ability to focus on the present moment, which can serve as a powerful distraction from pain and discomfort. When individuals experience chronic pain, their minds often become preoccupied with negative thoughts and worries about their condition.

Mindfulness encourages a shift in focus, allowing you to redirect your attention to your breath, bodily sensations, becoming highly aware of yourself and your thoughts and feelings. This practice can create a buffer against the emotional and psychological toll of pain you are experiencing, allowing you to feel in control of your pain experience rather than having it control you.

Incorporating mindfulness into your daily routine is easy to achieve, once you have learnt simple techniques, such as meditation, guided imagery, and visualisation practices. These methods will enable you to engage with your inner thoughts and feelings in a constructive manner.

For instance, guided imagery can help create mental images that promote relaxation and comfort, while visualisation can facilitate a sense of empowerment and control over your pain experiences.

By integrating these techniques into your life, you can develop a more mindful approach to managing pain and discomfort.

A simple mindfulness activity requires just five minutes and can be used at any time of the day. It does not require any special equipment or a specific environment. You can be sat on a bus, at work, anywhere, just be sure not to be driving. It is so simple, you just take a deep breath in, to the count of five; one, two, three, four and five. Now, hold that breath, to the count of one, two and three.

Now, release that breath, to the count of one, two, three, four and five. You may want to close your eyes and visualise calming imagery, such as a tropical beach or a cascading waterfall. Continue for just five minutes and you will find yourself becoming calmer, thoughts becoming quieter, and your sense of pain shifting and dulling.

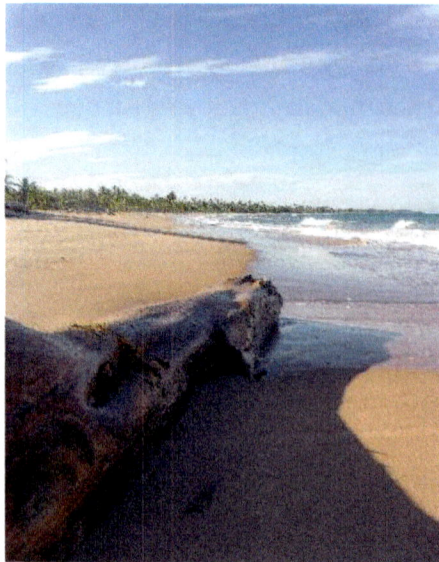

Creativity plays a crucial role in enhancing our mindfulness practice. Engaging in artistic activities, such as painting, music, or writing, provides an outlet for expression and self-discovery. These activities can help you to immerse yourself in the present moment, allowing for a deeper connection to your emotions and experiences.

Journaling and writing in particular, serves as an effective coping mechanism, enabling you to process your thoughts and feelings, as Rogers' use of self-reflection also suggests. In this case, writing is a tool to reflect on your pain and how you experience your disabilities and/or chronic conditions. This creative exploration can foster a sense of agency and resilience, further enhancing the benefits of mindfulness.

Finally, to define mindfulness in the context of pain management, one must recognise its multifaceted nature. It is not merely a practice but it should become a way of living, which can facilitate your self-awareness, acceptance, and understanding of how to manage your pain experiences.

For individuals facing the challenges of disabilities, chronic conditions, or significant life transitions, mindfulness offers a pathway to navigate your experiences with greater ease and understanding. By embracing mindfulness and its associated techniques, you can transform your pain journey and master your relationship with pain.

Benefits of Mindfulness for Chronic Pain

Mindfulness offers a transformative approach when dealing with chronic pain. One of the most significant benefits of mindfulness as mentioned, is its ability to distract the brain from the relentless focus on pain.

By helping you to live in the present moment, mindfulness can redirect attention away from any discomfort and towards more positive experiences. This shift in focus can create a space where pain feels less dominant, allowing for a greater sense of control and well-being.

Incorporating mindfulness techniques into your daily routine can put you firmly in control of pain management by fostering a deeper awareness of bodily sensations and emotional responses.

Mindfulness practices such as meditation and deep breathing will enable you to observe your pain without fear, reducing the anxiety and stress that often accompany chronic conditions.

This non-reactive observation can diminish the perceived intensity of pain and improve your overall emotional resilience, empowering you to respond to pain with greater calm and clarity.

As a psychologist, I trained in hypnobirthing eighteen years ago, while also being a hypnotherapist. In my work, I have personally witnessed and used powerful mindfulness practices. A key problem with pain is that the pain experienced, can trigger ongoing and accumulative stress. If we know we will experience pain, we feel stressed and anxious and this then places us in the 'Fight or Flight' response in how we manage our pain experiences. Stress hormones released in the Fight mode, can enhance our sense of strength and power, enhancing our ability to cope with pain . We may push through the pain, taking painkillers and treatments to cope, only to find at a later point, when the stress hormones decrease, we experience even more pain.

In the Flight response, we try to avoid all known triggers that can cause the pain, In my case, I would avoid temperature fluctuations increased my risk of experiencing pain. Hence, in flight mode as a response to experienced pain, I would avoid going outside in cold weather, but this in turn exacerbated my stress, as I would miss the joy of social engagements and upset friends and family, in declining their invitations. Hence, whether we adopt the flight or fight response in response to experienced pain, it is not an effective way of managing pain in the long-term, for a number of reasons. Firstly, if we adopt the Fight approach, we may come to rely on the use of painkillers to manage pain and place ourselves at risk of developing addiction issues. If we adopt a Flight response, then we may avoid doing activities that we once enjoyed, which could foster resentment, upset and frustration.

Thirdly, if we manage pain by continuously employing the fight or flight response, we will trigger a constant release of stress hormones on our bodies. Research reveals that stress hormones, experienced on a long-term basis, can increase the risk of experiencing cardiovascular, musculoskeletal, cognitive and metabolic issues. Hence, accumulation of stress hormones will increase our risk also of experiencing additional chronic and life-limiting conditions. Hence, it is vital to find more effective methods of pain management that stop the fight or flight response from releasing stress hormones. This is where mindfulness is your friend.

In my hypnotherapy practice, at the beginning of a session, I would draw on mindfulness practice to aid a client to enter a calm and relaxed state. Try this mindfulness activity, but before you start, write down on a scale of 1 to 10; what intensity level your experienced pain is, at this very moment. This activity is best if you can find a place to sit or lie down, it can be quiet or you can listen to relaxing music. I want you to get relaxed, arms by your side and close your eyes.

Breathe in to the count of one, two, three, four and five, then out to the count of one, two, three, four and five. Now keep repeating. I want you, as you breathe in and out, to imagine all the muscles in your body are relaxing, starting with your shoulders, arms, then hands, next, your head, neck, chest, stomach, legs and feet, Then, you will feel all the muscles in your face, eyes and chin gently relaxing, melting away into calm.

When all your body is relaxed, you may find you are no longer thinking about your breathing and that is fine, you are relaxed.

Next, imagine a winding road. You are walking along that road, the road is made of gravel, you can almost feel it beneath your feet. To the side of the road are corn fields and the corn towers high around you. The sky is blue, while the sun is warm and its rays are soothing on your skin. Continue to walk down this road and let your mind take you on a journey down it. The journey is for you to create, where does the road lead? Do you see familiar faces along the way? When you are ready you will reach the end of the road and open your eyes, feeling a sense of calm and peacefulness.

Keep practicing this mindfulness activity for around ten to fifteen minutes each day. Each time you open your eyes, reflect on how you feel and rate your pain on a level of one to ten. With practice, you will find that you can learn to actively reduce your pain levels.

Alongside using mindfulness activities as stand alone strategies in pain management, combining these within creative activities can serve as a powerful tool for enhancing the mindfulness approach in pain management. Engaging in for example, colouring, is a very simple method that can support you in quickly attaining a state of calm, both physically and mentally. This form of expression not only provides a distraction but can improve mood and emotional well-being.

I recommend the use of adult colouring books, colouring is not just for children and can be integrated with the breathing techniques and mindfulness practices. This will help you to develop new coping strategies that resonate with your personal experiences of pain.

Guided imagery and visualisation practices as used on the minute mindfulness activity just undertaken, can also help you to be autonomous in escaping the grip of pain, by gaining the skills to envision a peaceful place or imagining your body free from discomfort. Such practices support relaxation, lower your stress levels, and promote a sense of control over your pain experience. Regular engagement in visualisation exercises will enhance the effectiveness of mindfulness, leading to improved pain management outcomes.

Meditation Techniques for Beginners

Meditation combined with mindfulness is a powerful tool for individuals managing disabilities and chronic conditions. It can help in coping with life transitions, stress and anxiety. For beginners, understanding different meditation techniques can ease the process of incorporating mindfulness into daily life.

The primary goal of meditation is to cultivate a sense of awareness and presence, which can help you to distract your mind from pain and discomfort. You can adapt various techniques like those in the last chapter, according to your preferences and needs, making meditation accessible and beneficial for a diverse audience.

One effective technique for beginners is focused breathing. In the last two activities, the breathing to the count of five is an example of this. Breath work is a simple practice that entails only paying attention to the rhythm of your breath. Find a comfortable position, then, close your eyes if you like, take a deep breath in through your nose, let your abdomen expand. Then, slowly let that breath out, gently through your mouth. Focusing only on the release of that breath. This creates a calming effect, allowing your thoughts about pain or discomfort to drift away. This technique is very beneficial if you are experiencing acute pain, as it provides an immediate tool to regain control over your mental state.

Body scan meditation is another technique to consider. This practice encourages awareness of physical sensations throughout the body, helping you to connect with areas of tension or discomfort. To begin, lie down in a comfortable position or sit with a straight back. Start at your toes, noticing any feelings of tension or relaxation, and gradually move upward through your entire body.

This approach can foster a deeper understanding of how pain manifests physically, leading to a greater sense of acceptance and ease. Regular practicing body scans can help individuals learn to release tension and promote relaxation.

Guided imagery as noted in the ten to fifteen minute mindfulness activity undertaken earlier, is a powerful method that can enhance meditation for beginners. By visualising calming scenes or engaging in mental storytelling, you can create a mental escape from pain and stress.

Continue to practice guided imagery, find a quiet space and either listen to a recorded session or visualise a peaceful place, such as a beach or a serene forest. As you immerse yourself in the details of this scene—the sounds, smells, and sights—you can cultivate a sense of peace that can help alleviate your feelings of pain. This technique not only serves to distract your mind but can also promote a sense of well-being and tranquility.

Lastly, try incorporating journaling into your meditation practice; it can be an effective way to process your thoughts and emotions. After a meditation session, take a few moments to write down any feelings or insights that arose. This practice can help in recognising patterns in your pain experiences and emotional responses, providing a creative outlet for self-reflection.

Journaling can also serve as a coping mechanism, allowing you to articulate your experiences and track your progress over time. Combining meditation with writing can deepen your overall experience, making mindfulness a dynamic part of your daily life.

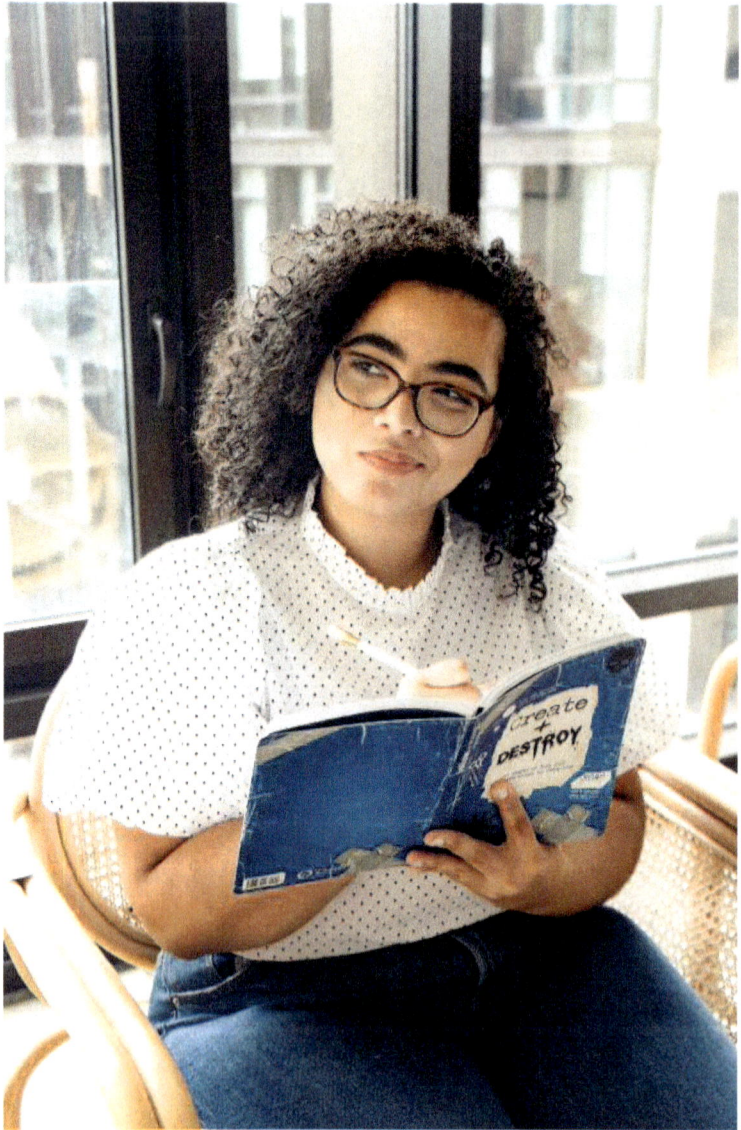

Chapter 3: Creativity Techniques

Overview of Creativity

Creativity can utilise various artistic modalities, such as drawing, painting, sculpting, dancing, singing, acting, scrapbooking, sewing. The list is endless and all can be drawn upon to promote healing and well-being. Creativity is a therapeutic practice that encompasses many methods and genres, to support you in finding a unique outlet for self-expression. For people with disabilities and chronic conditions, as well as those navigating significant life transitions such as menopause or pregnancy, creativity can serve as a vital tool in managing anxiety, stress, pain and fostering emotional resilience. By engaging in creative processes, you can distract your mind from discomfort, providing you with a sense of control and empowerment.

One of the main principles of being creative as discussed earlier, is, its ability to facilitate a space for mindfulness, allowing you to focus on the present moment. Mindfulness practices are essential for individuals dealing with chronic pain, as they help in reducing anxiety and depression that often accompany such conditions.

Through engaging in artistic activities, you can learn to actively cultivate a state of awareness that diverts your attention away from your experienced pain and towards the enjoyment of the creative process. This shift can lead to improved emotional states and a greater capacity to cope with challenges.

In addition to mindfulness, creativity can incorporate techniques such as guided imagery and visualisation practices. These approaches allow you to actively create mental images that evoke feelings of comfort and relaxation.

In creative activities, such as drawing, painting and sculpting, visualisation is at a physical level, where your mind can physically recreate your images in a form of media; facilitating self-expression and awareness.

By visualising positive experiences or serene landscapes and then recreating these within creative activities, you can enhance your ability to manage pain by refocusing your awareness. This technique not only distracts the mind but also promotes relaxation, resulting in a reduction in physical symptoms associated with stress and discomfort.

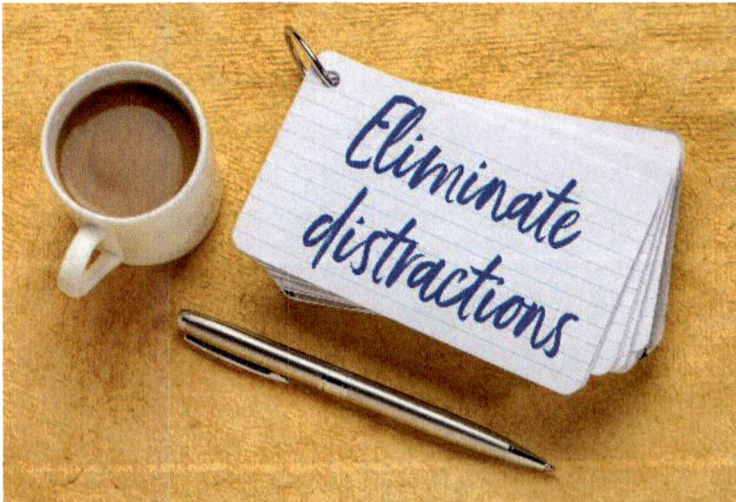

If you prefer the use of words rather than art imagery, Journaling and writing have become essential components of being creative, offering a profound way for you to express and process your experiences and emotions. Try this activity, open your journal and express gratitude. Write down three things you are thankful for today. Next, close your eyes and note how these three things make you feel. Go back into your journal and write down your feelings. Note how your awareness is no longer focused on the pain,

By articulating your thoughts and feelings, you can reduce not only the experienced pain but also negative thinking patterns. In refocusing on positive thoughts and feelings, you will feel more positive and be able to cope with your pain experience. The act of writing can be therapeutic in itself, allowing for the release of pent-up emotions and fostering a sense of connection to one's inner self.

Overall, being creative provides a multifaceted approach to pain management that is particularly beneficial for those facing disabilities, chronic conditions, and significant life changes.

By embracing creativity as a means of expression and healing, you can cultivate mindfulness, utilise visualisation techniques, and engage in reflective writing, all of which contribute to improved emotional and physical well-being. As this therapeutic practice continues to grow, it offers hope and healing for many seeking alternative avenues of support in their journeys toward managing pain and enhancing their quality of life.

Art as a Form of Expression

Art serves as a powerful form of expression, providing you with a unique outlet to communicate feelings and experiences that are often difficult to articulate verbally. Participants can channel their emotions through painting, drawing or other artistic endeavors turning abstract feeling into tangible forms that can lead to a better understanding of their experiences. Creativity therefore becoming a vital tool for emotional release and self-exploration. Engaging in creative practices will allow you to externalise your internal struggles, offering a sense of relief from pain and discomfort.

Through painting, drawing, or other artistic endeavors, you can channel your emotions, turning abstract feelings into tangible forms, which can lead to a greater understanding of your experiences. Its strange how as children, we are taught and encouraged to be creative and yet as adults, often, unless it is our career, we can place less value on it. We often think of self-care as going to a spa or having a bath with candles.

Creative activities however, are a valuable form of self-care. Simply carrying a colouring book or art pad in your bag and colouring or scribbling at the bus stop or on the train, can do wonders for our mental health and stress levels. Creativity needs to become part of our daily routine and lives.

These brief creative moments can facilitate small mindfulness activities, to ensure you maintain calm throughout the day.

It can make you better able to cope with the daily stressors that often enter our lives. This practice invites you to focus on the process of creating rather than the outcome, which can be particularly beneficial for those managing chronic pain or other health challenges.

By immersing yourself in brief artistic activities, you can distract your mind from pain, helping you to keep your pain experiences at a perceived lower level - preventing them from increasing to higher levels. This mindful engagement not only provides distraction but also cultivates a deeper connection to your body and emotions, enhancing overall well-being.

In this next activity, I want you to get in tune with your inner child. Remember a time when you engaged in creative play. How did you express yourself in art as a child?. Did you like to finger paint perhaps?.

Take an A4 sheet of paper and some tubes of acrylic paint. Now take three colours and pour paint from each tube into a pot. Do this for each colour. Now, dip your fingers in the paint.

Really think about how the paint feels on your fingers, is it cold or wet. squidgy? When you are focusing on the sensation of paint on your fingers, what happens to the sensation of pain? Has it changed perhaps?

Now express yourself on the paper, what you create is entirely your decision, just have fun creating.

After you have created your art, I want you to reflect on the activity. In your journal, write how doing this activity made you feel? Did it change your perception of pain?. How did you feel after you completed your picture? What have you learnt from this? Will you do this again?

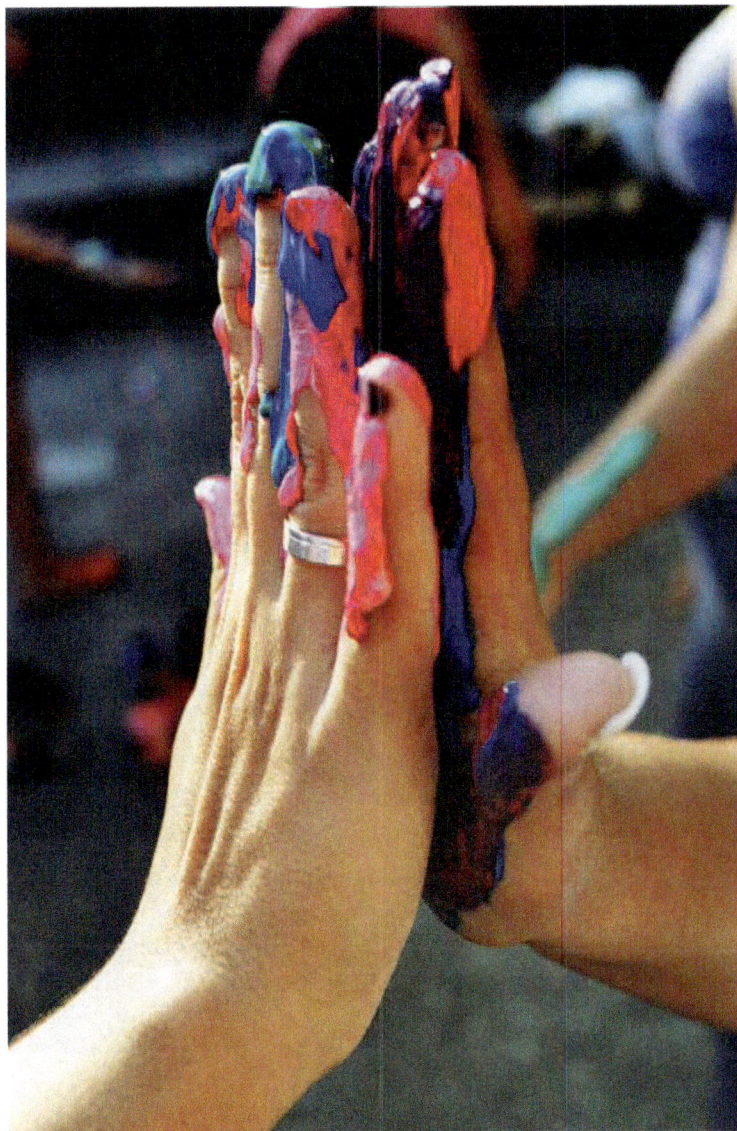

While art as a form of expression can give you the self care tools to empower you to reclaim your own pain narrative. By allowing your inner child to be creative by engaging in creative arts, you may find you can also become more attuned to your own emotions and needs.

This process of creating can become a journey of healing, offering not just distraction from pain, but also a pathway to mindfulness, self-discovery, and resilience. Through art, you can find solace, connection, and empowerment, transforming your experiences into something meaningful, enjoyable and beautiful.

Colouring books and their Benefits

Colouring books have emerged as popular tools for relaxation and mindfulness, offering a creative outlet that can be particularly beneficial for individuals with disabilities and chronic conditions, as well as those negotiating life transitions. Engaging in the simple act of colouring can allows you to become totally immersed in a world of creativity, fostering a sense of calm that can divert attention away from your pain and discomfort. This form of artistic expression not only provides a distraction but also encourages a focus on the present moment, making it an effective practice ,if your seeking relief from chronic pain or stress.

One of the primary benefits of colouring books is their ability to offer a quick methods of promoting mindfulness. You can easily access creative, self care activities, by carrying books in your bags or placing them on side tables in your living room. The repetitive motion of colouring can induce a meditative state, allowing you to concentrate on the task at hand, rather than your pain or worry. This focused attention can help to ground you, making it easier to navigate challenging emotions and physical sensations. By incorporating mindfulness into the colouring process, you can create a sanctuary of calm amidst the chaos of their experiences, enhancing your overall emotional well-being.

Colouring also serves as a form of creativity, which can be particularly advantageous when you are managing pain.

The act of choosing colours and applying them to a page can stimulate the brain's reward pathways, releasing endorphins that contribute to a sense of happiness and relief. This therapeutic aspect of colouring can be particularly appealing to those who find other forms of physical activity challenging, due to their conditions. Furthermore, the creative expression involved in colouring can empower you, fostering a sense of agency in a time when you may feel limited by your circumstances.

In addition to its therapeutic benefits, colouring can enhance coping mechanisms through guided imagery and visualisation practices. As you colour intricate designs and patterns, you can visualise peaceful scenes or positive affirmations that resonate with your healing journey. This combination of artistic expression and imaginative visualisation can help you, to create a powerful mental landscape, which encourages relaxation and pain management.

By integrating these practices into your daily routine, you can cultivate a more resilient mindset when facing the challenges of chronic pain or transitional life stages. There are many different forms of adult colouring books that can enable you to express your playful, humorous and even sarcastic side.

Finally, colouring books can serve as a valuable tool for journaling and reflection. By pairing colouring with written reflections or positive affirmations as our activity revealed, you can deepen your understanding of your emotions and experiences.

This dual approach not only allows for creative expression but also provides you with an opportunity for personal growth and insight. As you engage in this reflective practice, you may uncover new strategies for managing pain and stress, ultimately leading to a more empowered and mindful approach to managing your overall well-being.

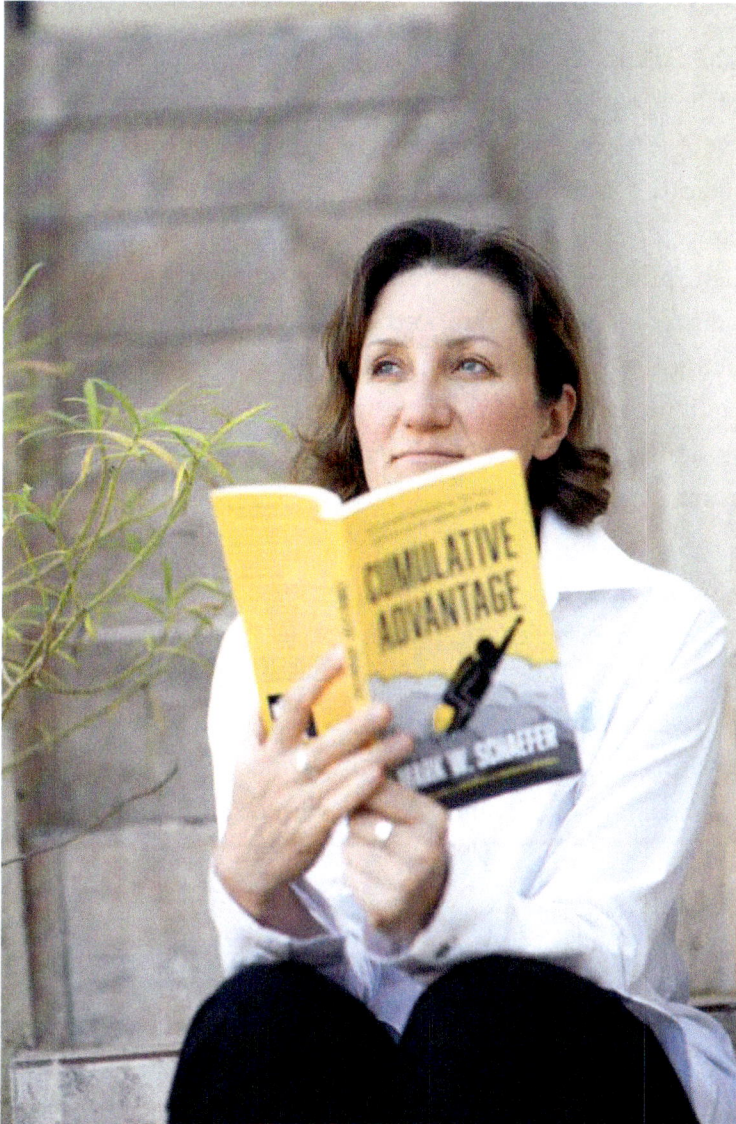

Chapter 4: Distracting the Brain: Techniques and Strategies

The Science of Distraction

The Science of Distraction is founded on an understanding of how our brain processes pain and how external stimuli can shift our focus away from discomfort. Research indicates that when we engage in activities that require concentration or creativity, our brains can inhibit the perception of pain. This concept is particularly beneficial in managing chronic conditions or navigating the physical and emotional challenges associated with menopause or childbirth. By harnessing the power of distraction, we can create a buffer against pain, allowing for a more manageable experience.

Our brains whilst complex are also in some ways quite simple. Ever tried to remember a shopping list of ten items in your head and then when you arrive in the shop, you can only remember five items. Competing information can distract our minds, leading to the replacement of past information with new information.

When you arrive at the shop, after having a conversation with a friend on the way, past information has been replaced by new information.

This is a rather simplistic explanation, but basically, if you give your brain competing information or in this case, other 'things' to attend to, your brain struggles to maintain attention on both past and more recent information. Hence, if we can purposely distract our brain by providing it with new incoming information, it can place less focus on the sensory information coming from the pain signals.

Distraction techniques can take many forms, from mindfulness practices as discussed, to creative activities and journaling, indeed to any form of activity. Mindfulness encourages you to focus on the present moment, which can reduce your intensity of pain experienced by redirecting attention away from the discomfort. This can be achieved through using the deep-breathing exercises or guided meditations undertook earlier in this book to promote relaxation. Creativity, in contrast, allows you to express your emotions and experiences through various artistic mediums, providing an outlet that not only distracts, but also fosters emotional healing.

Incorporating these distraction techniques into your daily routines can significantly enhance your quality of life as you learn to self-managing your chronic pain or navigate your life transitions. By understanding the science behind distraction and its impact on pain perception, you can develop personalised strategies that not only mitigate discomfort but also foster a deeper sense of mindfulness and creativity. By embracing these practices, you can open the door to a more peaceful existence, allowing you to craft calm amidst the challenges you face.

Incorporating creativity in our lives

So, the question is how can you incorporate creativity into your life? The good news is, it is simple to do and easily achievable. You do not have to be a budding artist or talented at all, because the benefit is not in the end product created, but the process of being creative.

Being creative is neither expensive or time consuming and can fit quite easily into your work and/or homelives. You can be creative independently, with family, friends, children, or as part of a community group. The opportunities to be creative in our daily lives are numerous, in the way we cook, dance to music, sing as we do the housework, there are so many ways to be creative.

Creativity is one of the most powerful and easy tools we can harness, in managing pain, anxiety, and/or the emotional challenges associated with living with disabilities, chronic conditions, menopause, pregnancy or childbirth. Engaging in creative activities daily can ensure that you make time for self care, allowing you to shift your focus away from your physical sensations and instead focus on simply being and doing.

This redirection censures you are in control, feel autonomous and can navigate your chronic health issues. It is often the feeling of not being in control that causes anxiety, increases stress and subsequently triggers pain experiences. Simple creative outlets, such as drawing, painting, or crafting, provide a sanctuary where the mind can explore new possibilities whilst your body finds a moment of respite.

Follow the simple mindfulness activities in this book, learn to breathe mindfully, learn how to create a space for calm and creativity each day and keep practicing to amplify their benefits. For example, practicing mindful drawing or coloring can enhance the meditative experience and with repeated practice, it will become easier to enter a calm and pain reduced state each time.

This engagement will not only calm your mind, but you will retain a sense of calm through the day, helping you to manage your disabilities, conditions or life transitions.

The products of your creativity, whether this be writing in your journal, paintings, drawings, pottery or something else, will also serve as a reminder of what you can achieve and have accomplished, as you learn to be mindfully creative.

Journaling and writing can serve as additional avenues for incorporating creativity into your daily life. In, putting pen to paper, a cathartic release can take place, enabling you, to process your experiences and emotions.

Writing about your pain management and life experiences, can create a sense of order and clarity amidst chaos. This practice can be particularly beneficial for menopausal women or new mothers navigating a whirlwind of changes, as it provides a safe space to reflect and articulate your journeys. This will foster a deeper appreciation for the creative process itself. By focusing on the act of creation rather than the discomfort, you will cultivate a sense of peace and tranquility, essential for emotional and physical well-being.

In learning how to be mindfully creative, you can build your own structured approach to utilising creativity for pain management. Through building on the guided activities in this book, you can further extend them, with new visualisations, adding sensory factors, such as fragrance or music and by testing what forms of creativity work for you.

You can explore various artistic mediums, allowing self-expression to flow freely. This therapeutic process encourages and enables you to communicate your feelings and experiences in ways that may have been difficult before, when using traditional dialogue. You will not only gain insights into how to cope and manage your pain, by articulating emotions through art, but also develop more effective and additional coping strategies.

The advantage of adopting a creative, mindful approach is that it can also be an effective adjunct therapy to prescribed medications that you may be taking; developing a multifaceted and individualised approach. By incorporating these techniques into your daily routines, you can not only manage pain more effectively, but also cultivate a rich tapestry of creativity, which will enhance your overall quality of life. Embracing creativity as a vital component of healing that will transform challenges you experience into opportunities for personal growth and self-discovery.

Chapter 5: Guided Imagery and Visualisation Practices

What is Guided Imagery?

Guided imagery is a therapeutic technique that involves using mental images to promote relaxation, reduce pain, and foster a sense of well-being. You were introduced earlier in the visualisation activities to it, when you imagined yourself on a winding road. It is often employed in various settings, including healthcare, to help individuals cope with chronic conditions, manage stress, and enhance their overall quality of life.

By engaging with your imagination, guided imagery allows you to visualise peaceful scenes, healing processes, or personal goals, effectively distracting your mind from pain and discomfort. This practice can be especially beneficial for people with disabilities, chronic conditions, experiencing stress, anxiety or facing challenges in their lives.

At its core, guided imagery taps into the power of the mind-body connection. The brain responds to images and thoughts in ways that can evoke physical sensations, making it possible to influence the body's responses to pain and stress. For example, when someone imagines a serene beach or a lush forest, their body may begin to relax, heart rate may decrease, and tension may dissipate. This physiological response can serve as a critical tool for managing pain, as it provides a non-pharmacological method to access relief and comfort.

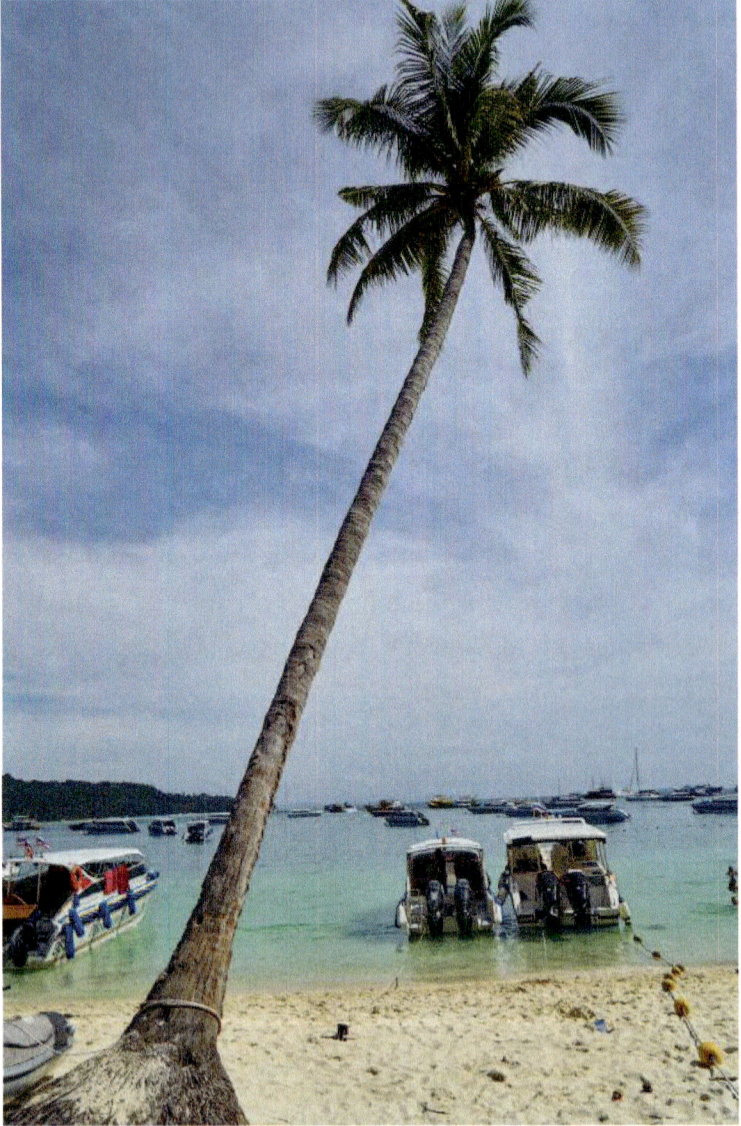

Guided imagery is typically facilitated by a trained therapist or through audio recordings, allowing you to engage fully in the experience. During a session, you are encouraged to close your eyes, take deep breaths, and focus your attention on the imagery being presented, such as the tropical beach on the prior page. As you visualise, you can incorporate sensory details such as sights, sounds, and smells, which can enhance your experience and promote deeper relaxation.

This immersive practice can also be tailored to your individual needs, making it a versatile approach suitable for a diverse audience. For example, adding wave sounds or lighting a scented candle can evoke a relaxing environment in which you can engage in guided imagery.

For those dealing with chronic pain or the effects of menopause, guided imagery can serve as a valuable coping mechanism. It offers a way to regain a sense of control over your body and emotions, reducing feelings of helplessness.

Additionally, new mothers can use guided imagery techniques during childbirth to visualise gently floating in the sea, helping to feel calm, alleviate anxiety and promote a smoother labour process. By integrating guided imagery into their daily routines, you can cultivate mindfulness and resilience in the face of challenges.

An activity to use in 'dialing down' pain using guided imagery, is to imagine in your mind, a dial with numbers 1-5, as you breathe in and out to the count of one, two, three, four and five, you visualise turning the dial down from 5 to 4. As you turn the dial, you imagine your body and mind becoming calmer. You continue to breathe in and out, turning the dial each time, from 4 to 3, 3 to 2 and 2 to 1. Repeating the same process until you reach one and your perceived pain decreasing with the turning of the dial.

This is a simple guided imagery technique, using mindfulness and breathing, once learned however, you will be able to dial down your pain when needed,

Techniques for Effective Visualisation

As you become more familiar with visualisation techniques, you will understand what powerful tools they are in managing pain and living well with disabilities, chronic conditions, and adjusting to life's transitions and challenges. Effective visualisation entails creating vivid mental images that can help you to distract the mind from discomfort, promote relaxation, and foster a sense of control over your body and experiences. By engaging and becoming immersed in imagination, you can cultivate a supportive mental environment that will aid you in managing pain and promoting emotional well-being. In this way, visualisation is another form of creativity, as when you become more familiar with mindfulness and visualisation techniques, you will be able to create your own visualisation techniques and imagery.

Developing your own guided imagery can be like creating little 'films' in your mind. This technique requires you to conjure up a calming scene or scenario that evoke feelings of peace and comfort. For example, imagining a serene beach, complete with the sound of waves and the warmth of the sun, can transport your mind away from pain and anxiety. Practitioners use recordings or scripts that help to lead you through these visualisations, ensuring you remain focused and engaged.

This process not only provides a mental escape but can also stimulate the body's relaxation response, reducing tension and discomfort. As you learn to use visualisation, you will be able to develop your own imagery, which will help you to quickly and easily achieve a state of calm and mindfulness, actively taking control of your mind, body and pain.

Incorporating mindfulness into visualisation practices does enhance its effectiveness in eliciting calm and managing pin. Mindfulness encourages individuals to remain present and aware of their thoughts and feelings without external distractions. This practice, when combined with visualisation, can deepen your relaxation experience. For instance, while visualising a peaceful landscape, you can focus on your breath, noticing how your chest rises then falls, as you inhale then exhale. This dual focus on the imagery and the breath creates a holistic approach to pain management, allowing for greater emotional regulation and stress reduction.

Examples of Guided Imagery Scripts

Guided imagery scripts can be a powerful tool for individuals managing chronic pain, or navigating life's challenges. These scripts serve as structured narratives that encourage relaxation and visualisation, allowing you to create mental images that foster a sense of calm and control. For people with disabilities and chronic conditions, guided imagery can help distract you from pain and discomfort, providing an alternative focus that can enhance overall well-being. Consider a guided imagery script as a narrative.

Write a story of where you feel you would be calm and at peace. Then close your eyes and imagine images that match the script you developed, using mindfulness and breath work, to become fully immersed in that imagery.

One effective guided imagery script might begin with you finding a comfortable position, either seated or lying down. The script could prompt you to take several deep, slow breaths, allowing tension to melt away with each exhale. As you guide yourself deeper into relaxation, you may tell yourself to visualise a serene landscape, such as a peaceful beach or a lush forest. This imagery can evoke feelings of safety and tranquility, helping you to shift attention away from pain and discomfort.

Another example of a guided imagery script focuses specifically on pain management. In this scenario, you could visualise your pain as a colour or shape, giving it a tangible form.

Your script asks you to imagine a warm, healing light enveloping that pain, gradually transforming its color or size. This visualisation technique can empower you to feel more in control of your pain experience, allowing you to manipulate your perception of discomfort through mental imagery.

For women experiencing menopause, a guided imagery script can address any feelings of anxiety and discomfort associated with hormonal changes. Your script could guide you to envision a soothing waterfall, with each drop of water representing a wave of relief washing over you. As you immerse yourself in this imagery, you can visualise your body becoming lighter and more relaxed, helping to alleviate any feelings of tension and stress that may accompany your menopausal symptoms.

A guided imagery script can foster a sense of empowerment and calm in childbirth. As an expectant mother, you can be guided to visualise a safe, warm environment where you feel supported and strong. The script can encourage you to imagine each contraction as a wave, reminding you that you have the strength to ride through it. This imagery can create a positive mindset, allowing you to approach labor with confidence and reduce any feelings of fear or anxiety. By developing and personalising your own guided imagery scripts, you can promote relaxation and effective pain management by utilising your creativity and imagination.

Chapter 6: Journaling and Writing as Coping Mechanisms

The Therapeutic Benefits of Journaling

Journaling has emerged as a powerful tool for individuals facing various challenges, such as life transitions, disability and various health conditions. As discussed earlier, this therapeutic practice offers a structured way to express emotions, thoughts, and experiences, serving as an outlet for the pent-up feelings that often accompany physical discomfort or emotional distress. By putting pen to paper, you can confront your pain and anxiety, creating a safe space to explore your inner worlds without judgment.

One of the primary therapeutic benefits of journaling is its ability to foster mindfulness. When you engage in writing, you are encouraged to focus on your current thoughts and feelings, promoting a sense of presence that can be particularly beneficial during times of stress or discomfort. This mindfulness practice helps to ground you, allowing you to step back from your pain and observe it rather than become overwhelmed by it. Through this process, journaling can shift the focus away from physical sensations, helping to distract your brain and reduce perceptions of pain.

Additionally, journaling serves as a method of emotional release. Chronic pain and life-altering conditions often come with a whirlwind of emotions, including frustration, sadness, and fear.

Writing about these feelings can help you process your experiences and validate your emotions. This cathartic practice not only helps in understanding and accepting your situation but also in finding clarity and perspective. As you articulate your thoughts, you may uncover underlying issues or patterns that contribute to the perceived pain, paving the way for more informed coping strategies.

For example, we can develop patterns of negative thinking that can foster a self-fulfilling prophecy. If we tell ourselves that we will experience severe pain, we are directing our mind to look for that pain and hence, our focus on the pain will increase, due to our expectation that it will be intense pain.

Consequently, journaling can enhance self-reflection and self-awareness, by bringing into our consciousness these flawed and faulty thinking patterns, so that we can turn negative thinking into more positive thinking patterns, which support well being. By maintaining a regular writing practice, you can identify these thoughts, to implement change, to stop thinking pain will be severe and instead, using positive affirmations to foster positive self beliefs, such as 'I can control my pain' and/or 'My pain can be managed'.

You can also use journaling to identify triggers for pain or discomfort, and recognise achievements—no matter how small. This self-awareness will foster a sense of empowerment, allowing you to take an active role in your pain management journey. Over time, the insights gained through journaling can lead to a more profound understanding of yourself, your relationship with pain, and ability to effectively manage it. Ultimately this will encourage more effective coping mechanisms and behaviors.

Incorporating journaling into a broader creativity approach will further amplify its benefits. Using the techniques learned from guided imagery and visualisation will complement your use of journaling, providing a holistic framework for pain management. By combining these methods, you can create a comprehensive and individualised toolkit that not only addresses your physical symptoms, but, also nurtures your emotional and mental well-being. Through the art of journaling, you can cultivate resilience, find solace, and reclaim your personal narrative in the face of adversity.

Different Journaling Techniques

One popular technique is expressive writing, which encourages you to write freely about your thoughts and feelings without worrying about grammar or structure. This method allows for a deep exploration of emotions, providing an opportunity to release pent-up feelings associated with chronic pain or life changes.

Expressive writing can be particularly beneficial also if you are navigating the complexities of life transitions, as it fosters self-reflection and emotional processing, helping you to articulate your experiences and validate your feelings..

Another effective journaling approach is gratitude journaling, which we touched upon earlier in our activities, where you focused on finding three things in your life to be thankful for.

Gratitude journaling shifts attention from pain and discomfort to moments of joy and appreciation, promoting a mindset of positivity. If you are living with chronic conditions, cultivating gratitude can enhance your overall well-being and resilience, making it easier to cope with daily challenges. By acknowledging small victories and moments of happiness, you can create a sense of balance amidst your struggles.

Visual journaling as discussed, is another technique that combines art and writing, allowing for a more holistic expression of your thoughts and feelings. This approach can be particularly appealing if you find it difficult to articulate your experiences through words alone. By incorporating drawings, sketches, or collage elements into your journals, you can tap into your creativity and express emotions that may be otherwise hard to verbalise. The act of creating can provide a meditative experience for you, enabling you to focus your mind and distract yourself from pain, while exploring their inner worlds.

Writing affirmations for Pain Management

We have touched briefly upon the use of positive affirmations, these can be a powerful tool for managing pain, stress and/or anxiety. Affirmations are positive, present-tense statements that help reframe your thoughts and beliefs, promoting a sense of empowerment and control. By crafting affirmations focused on pain management, you can shift your mindset, reduce anxiety, and foster a more positive outlook on your health journey.

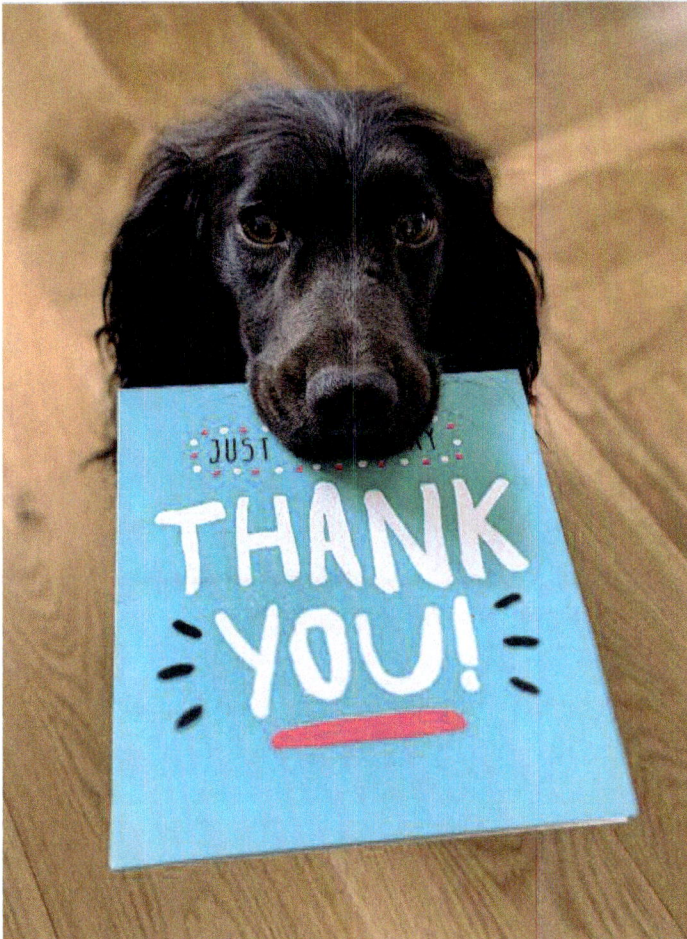

When formulating affirmations, it is essential to focus on the present moment and use language that resonates with you personally. Instead of saying, "I will not feel pain," a more effective affirmation might be, "I am in control of my body and my pain." This subtle shift emphasizes agency and acceptance rather than resistance. Affirmations should reflect personal experiences and aspirations, making them more meaningful and impactful. Tailoring affirmations to specific situations, such as managing discomfort during a menopausal hot flash or coping with labor pains, can enhance their relevance and effectiveness.

Incorporating mindfulness into the practice of writing affirmations can amplify their benefits. Before crafting affirmations, take a moment to center yourself through deep breathing or guided imagery. Visualising a calming scene or recalling a peaceful memory can help clear the mind and create a receptive state for writing. This mindful approach encourages deeper reflection on your feelings and experiences, allowing for the creation of affirmations that genuinely resonate with your current state and aspirations for pain management.

Journaling blends itself well with the affirmation-writing process. Keep a dedicated journal for affirmations, this allows you to track your thoughts, feelings, and responses to pain management strategies over time.

Reflecting on past affirmations can reveal patterns, helping you to identify which statements have been most effective.

Additionally, journaling about daily experiences with pain and how affirmations have influenced those experiences can enhance your understanding of the personal journey you have taken, towards managing pain through creative expression.

Finally, sharing affirmations with a supportive community, whether through group therapy, online forums, or with friends and family, can reinforce their power. Discussing affirmations not only provides encouragement but also opens the door for collaboration and the exchange of ideas. A collective approach to affirmations can foster a sense of belonging and validation, reminding you that you are not alone in your pain experiences and/or challenges. Embrace the practice of writing affirmations as part of a broader pain management strategy as this can lead to increased resilience, improved emotional well-being, and a more profound sense of calm in the face of pain.

Chapter 7: Integrating Techniques into Daily Life

Creating a Mindful Routine

Creating a mindful routine is essential. A mindful routine fosters a sense of control and stability, which can be particularly empowering when dealing with pain and uncertainty. By integrating mindfulness into daily activities, you can cultivate a greater awareness of your thoughts and feelings, allowing you to respond to discomfort with intention rather than reaction. Establishing a consistent routine requires not simply time management but also you creating a framework that supports your emotional well-being and pain management, through your developed mindful practices.

To begin crafting a mindful routine, it is important to identify specific activities that resonate personally. This may include the activities you have learned from this book, as well as meditation, deep breathing exercises, gentle stretching and guided imagery that you have personally developed. For those who may be less familiar with these practices, starting small can be effective. Setting aside just a few minutes each day to practice mindfulness can create a ripple effect, gradually increasing comfort and familiarity with these techniques. Over time, you can expand these routines by incorporating more varied guided imagery or visualisation, which can serve to distract the mind from pain and promote relaxation.

In addition to these practices, ensure to further your creativity, using different genres and media to foster a series of different mindful routines. This can enhance emotional expression and provide a constructive outlet for feelings associated with chronic pain or transitional life phases. It will also ensure you do not become bored with the same mindful routine. Engaging in activities such as drawing, painting, or writing can be both a distraction and a form of catharsis. Journaling, in particular, enables you to articulate your experiences and emotions, leading to insights that can enhance your mindfulness practice. By reflecting on daily challenges and triumphs, you can cultivate a deeper understanding of your pain and the context surrounding it.

Establishing a mindful routine also needs a supportive environment. Make sure to designate a specific space in the home for mindful practices, free from distractions. Enhancing this space with calming elements, such as soft lighting or soothing music, can further promote relaxation and focus. Additionally, consider setting reminders or cues throughout the day to engage in brief moments of mindfulness—such as pausing to breathe deeply or checking in with your body. These reminders can serve as anchors, gently guiding you back to the present moment when distractions arise.

Ultimately, a mindful routine is a personalised journey that evolves over time. Experiment with various practices and remain flexible as this will enable you to discover what works best for you. It is important to acknowledge that some days will be more challenging than others, and that's okay. The goal is to cultivate a sense of resilience through consistent practice, allowing mindfulness to permeate all aspects of your life.

By creating a mindful routine, you can empower yourself to navigate your experiences with greater ease, transforming pain management into a more holistic and compassionate process.

Setting Realistic Goals

Setting realistic goals is essential. Goals serve as a guide for personal growth and evaluating our successes in attaining pain management. Goals will help you to create a structured framework within which you can navigate your daily life. SMART goals are a great tool to help you focus your goals.

S stands for be specific; if you are not specific you set yourself up to fail. So, be clear about what your goals are. M is for measurable; what are you going to measure to know when you are achieving your goal. If your goal is to reduce pain, then the dial it down activity can be a good measure of whether you have succeeded in reducing your pain experience. The tools you need are in this book - so use them. R is for Realistic goals. Are your goal/s achievable and/or attainable?

If you have completed the activities in this book, you will be aware that a goal of managing pain is achievable. However, a goal to eliminate pain entirely may not be realistic, so it is important, how you phrase your goals, so that they are achievable. T is for time-bound; when setting goals, be specific about what time frame, you want to achieve your goal in. For example, you may set a time limit for a mindful routine of ten minutes each day, with the goal of minimising pain.

By emphasizing small, incremental changes rather than drastic expectations, you can maintain motivation and avoid the discouragement that can accompany unattainable aspirations. When you have set your SMART goals, you can develop your mindful routine with these criteria as the focus. These will assist you in developing your routine's content.

In the context of mindfulness and meditation, realistic goals can enhance the practice and make it more accessible. Instead of aiming for an hour of meditation every day, a more achievable goal could be to start with five minutes of guided imagery or visualisation techniques. This gradual approach will enable you to develop a regular practice without feeling pressured, which can lead to a greater sense of calm and control over your thoughts and feelings. As you become more comfortable, you can gradually increase the duration, reinforcing a positive cycle of achievement and relaxation.

Flexibility is another critical aspect of setting realistic goals. Chronic conditions or significant life changes, such as menopause or childbirth, can be unpredictable. Establishing goals that allow for adjustments when necessary can reduce stress and promote resilience. For example, if a journaling commitment of writing daily becomes too burdensome, you should feel empowered to modify it to a few times a week. This adaptability will support positive mental health and encourage continued engagement with creative outlets, even during challenging times.

In conclusion, setting realistic goals is a fundamental strategy for managing pain and enhancing well-being. By focusing on achievable objectives, you can create a personalised roadmap that acknowledges your unique challenges, while encouraging progress and self-compassion. Whether through creative arts, mindfulness practices, or journaling, these goals will foster a supportive environment for your personal expression and emotional healing.

By embracing a realistic approach, you can cultivate a more mindful and fulfilling life, even amidst adversity.

Evaluating Progress and Adjusting Practices

Evaluating progress in managing pain through the use of creativity and mindfulness, involves regular self-assessment and reflection. You will benefit from monitoring your emotional and physical responses to the various techniques you adopt. Regularly taking stock of what methods are effective,will allow you to reinforce positive practices, while identifying areas that may require adjustment.

Journaling can be an invaluable tool in this process, providing a space for you to note your feelings, triggers, and responses to different creative activities, thereby creating a personalised roadmap for your journey towards pain management.

A crucial aspect of evaluating progress is recognising the subtle shifts in your emotional and physical state. Mindfulness and meditation strategies encourage you to become aware of your thoughts and sensations without distraction. This state of awareness can reveal patterns and changes that might otherwise go unnoticed.

For example, you may discover that certain artistic practices, such as painting or drawing, help reduce anxiety levels on days when physical pain is more pronounced.

By fostering an environment of self-awareness, you can better understand the interplay between your emotional experiences and pain levels, leading to more tailored and effective coping strategies.

Adjusting practices based on evaluation can enhance the effectiveness of pain management approaches. If a particular method, such as guided imagery, is yielding limited results, exploring alternative techniques may be beneficial. You may find that integrating elements of creative arts, such as music or dance, complements your existing interests and strategies, providing new avenues for relief.

Flexibility in approach is essential; what works well at one time may not be as effective at another, especially as life circumstances and physical states evolve. Regularly revisiting and refining your creative and mindful practices ensures you remain engaged and responsive to your unique needs.

Support networks can play a vital role in this evaluative process. Engaging with others who share similar experiences can provide insights into successful techniques and practices.

Group art classes or engaging in the many online forums available, can help you to remain focused on exploring creative outlets in your pain management journey. It can also foster a sense of community, encouraging the sharing of strategies that have worked, so you can understand and share experiences, progress and challenges. Such interactions can inspire new ideas for coping mechanisms, as together you learn from each others' experiences. Collaboration and reflection on progress will not only enhance personal growth but will strengthen connection amongst participants.

Ultimately, the journey of evaluating progress and adjusting practices is an ongoing process. You must approach your pain management strategies with patience and openness, allowing for the possibility of change and adaptation over time.

By actively participating in this reflective practice, you can cultivate resilience and a sense of agency over your pain experience. The integration of mindfulness, creativity, and community support can create a holistic framework that empowers you to navigate your challenges with greater ease and confidence.

Chapter 8: Case Studies and Personal Stories

Success Stories from Individuals with Chronic Pain

Success stories from individuals living with chronic pain can serve as powerful reminders of resilience and the effectiveness of creative arts in managing discomfort. Many people with chronic conditions have found that engaging in artistic activities not only distracts them from their pain but also provides a sense of purpose and fulfillment.

For instance, Anne, who lives with fibromyalgia, discovered that painting allowed her to express her emotions in a constructive and healing way. Each brushstroke became a form of mindfulness, helping her to focus on the present moment rather than the chronic pain that often dominated her thoughts.

John, a retired teacher with arthritis, turned to journaling as a way to cope with his daily challenges. By documenting his experiences, he gained clarity and insight into his pain triggers, enabling him to make informed choices about his activities and self-care strategies. His journals became a source of strength, filled with reflections on gratitude and triumph over adversity. This practice not only alleviated his feelings of isolation but also fostered a sense of community as he shared his writings with others facing similar struggles.

Guided imagery and visualisation practices have proven effective for many dealing with chronic pain. Chris, living with multiple sclerosis utilised these techniques to create a mental sanctuary where he could mentally escape from his discomfort. By visualising a peaceful landscape, he learned to calm his mind and body, reducing his perception of pain. This practice not only aided in pain management but also encouraged a deeper connection to his inner self, allowing him to cope with the emotional aspects of his condition more effectively.

Mindfulness and meditation techniques have also played a crucial role in the narratives amongst individuals battling chronic pain. Sally, who was struggling as she navigated through menopause found solace in daily meditation. Meditation helped her manage not only physical discomfort but also emotional fluctuations. Through consistent practice, she developed a heightened awareness of her body and its signals, enabling her to respond to pain with compassion rather than frustration. Her story illustrates how mindfulness can create a buffer against pain, allowing for a more balanced and peaceful existence.

Lastly, the power of creative expression in therapy cannot be overstated. A group of individuals with chronic conditions came together to form an art therapy collective, where they shared their journeys through sculpture and collage. This collaborative environment fostered healing, camaraderie, and mutual support.

Each participant's unique story and artistic expression contributed to a shared understanding of pain, transforming their experiences into a source of collective strength. These success stories highlight the transformative potential of creative arts therapy, offering hope and inspiration to others navigating the complexities of chronic pain.

Experiences of Menopausal Women

Menopause is a major transitional period in a woman's life, often triggering a wide range of physical and emotional challenges. Women may experience symptoms, such as hot flashes, sleep disturbances, mood swings and cognitive changes. These experiences can be particularly intense for those with chronic conditions or disabilities, as the interplay between hormonal changes and existing health issues can exacerbate discomfort and emotional distress. Understanding these experiences is crucial for developing effective coping strategies that can ease the transition and improve quality of life.

Creative arts provide a holistic approach to managing the symptoms associated with menopause. Engaging in artistic activities such as painting, drawing, or music can serve as a powerful distraction from the discomfort of hot flashes or anxiety.

These creative outlets allow women to express their feelings and experiences in a safe space, helping to alleviate feelings of isolation that are comm during this phase. By focusing on the creative process rather than the symptoms, women can cultivate a sense of empowerment and control over their bodies and emotions.

Mindfulness and meditation techniques can also play a pivotal role in managing menopausal symptoms. Practicing mindfulness encourages women to stay present in the moment, reducing the tendency to ruminate on discomfort or negative feelings. Techniques such as deep breathing exercises or guided imagery can provide immediate relief during moments of distress.

Visualisation practices can help women imagine peaceful scenarios, promoting relaxation and reducing stress levels. Integrating these practices into daily routines can foster resilience, enabling women to navigate the challenges of menopause more effectively.

Journaling offers another invaluable tool for menopausal women. Writing about their experiences allows them to articulate their feelings, track symptoms, and identify triggers. This reflective practice not only serves as a coping mechanism but also helps women gain insight into their personal journeys.

By documenting their thoughts and experiences, they can identify patterns and develop strategies that work for them. Journaling can also create a sense of agency, transforming the menopause experience from one of suffering to one of self-discovery and growth.

Ultimately, the experiences of menopausal women are diverse and deeply personal. By embracing creativity, mindfulness techniques, and reflective practice, such as journaling, women can find effective ways to manage their symptoms and enhance their overall well-being.

These approaches foster a sense of community and connection, reminding women that they are not alone in their journey. Through creative expression and mindful practices, they can cultivate calm amidst the challenges of menopause, crafting a narrative that celebrates resilience and empowerment.

Lessons from Creative Visualisation in Childbirth

Creative visualisation has emerged as a powerful tool in managing pain and anxiety, particularly in the context of childbirth. Expectant mothers often face a myriad of fears and uncertainties as they approach labor.

By harnessing the principles of creativity, women can create mental images that foster a sense of calm and control. This technique allows them to visualise a safe and positive birthing experience, which not only helps reduces stress but also enhance the overall childbirth experience.

One of the key lessons from creative visualisation is the importance of mindset in pain management. Research indicates that the way individuals perceive pain can significantly alter their experience of it. When women engage in guided imagery, they can shift their focus from the anticipated discomfort of labor to empowering images of strength, safety, and support.

This mental shift can activate the body's relaxation response, which helps to mitigate pain and anxiety during labour.

Moreover, creative visualisation can be an effective complement to traditional pain management techniques. By combining visualisation with breathing exercises and mindfulness practices, women can create a holistic approach to managing labour pain.

For instance, visualising the rhythm of their breath as waves can help mothers maintain a steady focus, allowing them to navigate contractions with greater ease. This integrative approach not only promotes a sense of agency during childbirth but also cultivates a deeper connection to the birthing process itself.

Journaling and reflective writing play a crucial role in enhancing the effectiveness of creative visualisation. By documenting their fears, hopes, and experiences, expectant mothers can clarify their intentions for labour.

Writing can serve as a therapeutic outlet, helping to process emotions and visualise a positive outcome. This practice of self-expression not only empowers women to confront their anxieties but also reinforces their commitment to a mindful and intentional birthing experience.

Finally, the lessons learned from creative visualisation during childbirth extend beyond the delivery room. Individuals coping with disabilities or chronic conditions can apply similar techniques in their daily lives to manage pain and anxiety.

By visualising positive outcomes and engaging in mindful practices, they can cultivate resilience and empowerment in their personal journeys. The principles of creative visualisation offer a pathway towards not only alleviating pain but also embracing a more fulfilling life experience, regardless of the challenges faced.

Chapter 9: Resources for Continued Learning

Exploring the intersection of creativity and mindfulness can be immensely beneficial when managing chronic pain, disabilities, or the transitions of menopause and childbirth. There are numerous books and articles that delve into the therapeutic aspects of creative arts and mindfulness, providing valuable insights and practical techniques.

You will also find further books and courses on pain management, mindfulness, creativity and positive thinking alongside other health and wellbeing areas on my websites www.livingwellbooks.co.uk and at www.drjuliesacademy.co.uk

Incorporating further reading is an essential component of a well-rounded and effective personal wellness journey to enhance the understanding of how creativity and mindfulness intersect. The combination of practical exercises and theoretical insights allows individuals to cultivate new coping mechanisms and strategies for managing pain.

Furthermore, it can promote self-growth and offer profound insights into self-compassion, which is essential for anyone navigating the complexities of chronic conditions, menopause, or childbirth.

Finally, online platforms and blogs dedicated to creativity and mindfulness practices can provide ongoing support and community connections.

If you would like more information or to subscribe to my channels or newsletters, you will find me on TikTok, Facebook and Instagram @drjuliewinstanley. I regularly share posts and insights about issues relating to health and wellbeing, making these resources accessible to a broader audience.

Engaging with such content not only supports your continued individual learning and self development, but also fosters a sense of belonging among those facing similar challenges. By immersing yourself in these areas, you can harness the power of creative arts and mindfulness to craft your own path toward calm and pain management.

Online Courses and Workshops

Many online courses focus on mindfulness and meditation techniques, teaching you further methods to cultivate awareness and presence in your lives. These practices can be particularly beneficial for continuing to develop your mindful routines in managing pain. They will encourage you to redirect your focus away from discomfort and towards a state of calm.

Through guided sessions, you will further learn to harness your breath and body, creating a mental space that can significantly reduce your stress and anxiety, which are often exacerbated by chronic pain conditions. This approach not only empowers you to take control of your pain but also fosters resilience through self-awareness.

Creativity is a key component in the realm of online workshops. Visit my educational site www.drjuliesacademy.co.uk as I am continuously adding more classes and workshops in this area, to help support your personal pain management journey.

You will gain access to creative opportunities in the sessions available to explore various artistic mediums—such as painting, drawing, or music—to continue your self-expression and emotional release.

Engaging in creative activities can serve as a powerful distraction from physical pain, allowing you to immerse yourself in the process of creation. Workshops emphasize the therapeutic aspects of art, encouraging you to express your feelings, experiences, and struggles, which can lead to a sense of validation and connection to others facing similar challenges.

Guided imagery and visualisation sessions are also available alongside online courses, to further your skills and knowledge of tools to create mental images that will promote relaxation and healing. These techniques can be particularly effective for pain management, as they allow you to visualise yourself in a peaceful setting, enhancing your sense of control over the pain experience.

By further learning techniques to incorporate vivid imagery and positive affirmations in your mindful routine, you can cultivate new mental landscapes that will further support your healing journey. This will reinforce the mind-body connection essential for holistic well-being. Do visit www.drjuliesacademy.co.uk for details of events, classes and training in these areas.

Support Groups and Community Resources

Support groups and resources in your community play a vital role in offering support for your mental and emotional well-being, particularly, if you are also living with disabilities, chronic conditions, or navigating significant life transitions.

These groups provide a safe space for sharing experiences, fostering connections, and gaining insights from others, who understand the unique challenges faced. Engaging with support groups can alleviate feelings of isolation and empower you, by creating a sense of belonging and community.

You'll be amazed at how many creative opportunities exist in your local communities, often for free. Identify community resources in your area and utilise these to further enhance your creativity and mindfulness journey. Many communities offer workshops, classes, and events focused on mindfulness and meditation techniques.

These resources can equip you with valuable tools for managing pain and stress. Incorporating practices such as guided imagery and visualisation can empower you to take an active role in your pain management, fostering a sense of control and resilience.

To maximise the benefits of support groups and community resources, you must actively seek out and participate in these opportunities. By connecting with others who share similar experiences, you can learn from one another, share coping strategies, and discover new techniques for managing pain.

Engaging in these supportive environments can ultimately enhance your overall well-being, foster resilience, and promote a more mindful approach to living with chronic conditions or navigating significant life changes.

Chapter 10: Conclusion: Embracing a New Approach to Pain Management

The Journey To creativity and Mindful Living

The journey to creativity and mindful living is a transformative process that can significantly enhance your quality of life if you are living with disabilities, chronic conditions, or going through transitions such as menopause and childbirth.

At its core, this journey involves cultivating an awareness of the present moment while engaging in creative expression. This dual focus not only helps distract the brain from pain and discomfort, but also fosters a sense of empowerment and agency. By integrating mindfulness practices with creativity, you can develop a toolkit of strategies that promote emotional well-being and resilience.

Engaging in creativity provides a unique avenue for self-expression and exploration of feelings that may be difficult to articulate verbally. This process not only serves as a distraction from physical pain but also allows for the release of pent-up emotions, facilitating a deeper connection with self. As you immerse yourself in creative activities, you will often find that your mindfulness naturally increases, as you become fully present in the moment, focusing on the sensory experiences of your chosen medium.

Mindfulness and meditation techniques play a crucial role in your journey, offering additional layers of support for pain management and emotional regulation. Simple practices such as focused breathing, body scans, or guided meditations can be easily integrated into your daily routines.

These techniques encourage you to observe your thoughts and sensations without judgment, promoting a sense of calm and acceptance. When combined with creative expression, mindfulness practices can enhance the therapeutic effects, helping you to cultivate a compassionate relationship with your body and pain experiences.

Guided imagery and visualisation practices will further enrich your journey toward mindful living. By harnessing the power of imagination, you can create mental landscapes that promote relaxation and pain relief. Visualisations can be tailored to your personal preferences, allowing for a deeply individualised experience.

As you envision serene settings or empowering scenarios, your brain can trigger physiological responses that reduce tension and discomfort. This imaginative approach not only provides a coping mechanism for pain, but also reinforces the connection between your mind and body, essential for holistic well-being.

Journaling and writing serve as powerful coping mechanisms that complement creative activities and mindfulness practices. By putting thoughts and feelings on paper, you can gain clarity and insight into your experiences.

Journaling can be a reflective practice, allowing for the processing of emotions related to chronic pain, disability, or life transition experiences. Moreover, writing can serve as a form of storytelling, enabling you to reclaim your personal narrative and find meaning in your journey. Through these expressive outlets, the path to creativity and mindful living becomes not just a therapeutic practice but a deeply personal exploration of resilience and hope.

Encouragement for Continued Practice

Continued practice in creativity and mindfulness is essential for you to navigate the complexities of chronic conditions and disabilities. Engaging in creative activities can serve as a powerful distraction from pain, allowing your mind to focus on the process rather than the discomfort. When you immerse yourself in artistic endeavors, whether it be painting, drawing, or crafting, you activate different areas of your brain, promoting a sense of calm and reducing the perception of pain. This shift in focus not only helps in managing immediate discomfort but also cultivates a lasting resilience against the stressors associated with chronic health issues.

Mindfulness and meditation techniques are invaluable tools in this journey. By incorporating regular mindfulness practices into your routine, you can enhance your ability to cope with pain and stress.

Simple techniques such as deep breathing, body scans, or guided imagery can help ground you in the present moment, offering a reprieve from overwhelming sensations. As you practice mindfulness, you may find that your emotional responses to pain change, fostering a greater sense of control and acceptance. This transformation is crucial for those managing the unpredictable nature of chronic conditions and can lead to improved emotional well-being.

Creative arts also encourage emotional expression, which is vital for holistic healing. Journaling and writing can be particularly effective methods for processing feelings related to pain and disability. By putting pen to paper, you create a space for reflection, allowing yourself to explore and articulate your experiences.

This practice not only serves as an emotional outlet but it will also help you to identify patterns and triggers associated with your pain. Over time, journaling can become a cherished ritual that helps you document your journey, providing insight into your progress and resilience.

In addition to journaling, engaging in guided imagery and visualisation practices can enhance your coping mechanisms. These techniques allow you to create mental images that evoke feelings of safety, peace, and joy. By consistently practicing visualisation, you train your brain to access these calming images during moments of pain or distress, effectively altering your body's response to discomfort. This mental rehearsal can be a powerful adjunct to your pain management toolkit, fostering a sense of empowerment and agency over your experience.

Encouragement for continued practice should focus on the gradual integration of these techniques into daily life. Start with small, manageable sessions of creative expression or mindfulness exercises, gradually increasing the duration as you become more comfortable. Celebrate your progress, no matter how minor, and remind yourself that consistency is key.

By committing to these practices, you are not only nurturing your creative spirit but also building a robust foundation for managing pain and enhancing your overall quality of life. Embrace the journey, and allow yourself the grace to evolve as you explore the therapeutic benefits of creativity.

Final Thoughts on Creativity and Pain Management

Creativity serves as a powerful tool for individuals dealing with chronic pain and various conditions. By engaging in creative activities such as art, music, and writing, individuals can redirect their focus away from discomfort and toward self-expression and exploration. This shift in attention is crucial for pain management, as it allows individuals to temporarily escape their physical experiences and immerse themselves in the therapeutic process. The act of creating not only distracts the mind but also promotes a sense of accomplishment and control, which is particularly beneficial for those navigating the challenges of disability or chronic conditions.

Mindfulness plays a significant role in becoming and being creative, as it encourages you to be present in the moment without judgment. This approach helps you to cultivate awareness of your thoughts and feelings while engaging in creative activities. Techniques like guided imagery and visualisation can help to improve this experience. By visualising peaceful scenes or imagining a life free from pain, you can invoke a sense of calm and relaxation. These practices foster a deeper connection between the mind and body, making it easier for you to manage your pain and emotional responses.

Journaling and writing serve as effective coping mechanisms within the framework of creative arts therapy. For many individuals, expressing thoughts and feelings through writing can lead to insights and a better understanding of their pain.

By engaging within a reflective process can help you to articulate your experiences, identify triggers, and explore your emotional landscape. By documenting your journey, you can create a narrative that empowers you to take control of your story, ultimately aiding you in managing pain and promoting emotional healing.

For menopausal women and those experiencing childbirth, creativity and mindfulness offer unique benefits. The hormonal changes and physical challenges faced during these life stages can evoke feelings of anxiety and discomfort. Engaging in creative practices can provide an outlet for these emotions, allowing for a more positive experience. Whether through painting, crafting, or music, these activities can promote relaxation and foster a sense of community, especially when shared with others facing similar challenges. This sense of connection can be invaluable in managing pain and enhancing overall well-being.

In conclusion, creativity and mindfulness stand as a versatile and effective approach to pain management. By combining mindfulness, distraction techniques, and self-expression, you can find relief from your pain experience, whilst nurturing your emotional and mental health. This holistic approach not only addresses the physical aspects of pain but also empowers you in actively reclaiming control over your life and fostering resilience. As more people explore the integration of creative practices into their pain management strategies, the potential for improved quality of life becomes increasingly attainable.

The End

Be Creative
and
dial that pain down!

Printed in Great Britain
by Amazon